HOW TO FUCK OFF!
IN 50 LANGUAGES

Compiled by
Kelvin Birdseye

OLD ROPE BOOKS
AN IMPRINT OF JOHN BROWN PUBLISHING

First published in Great Britain in November 1993 by
John Brown Publishing Ltd, The Boathouse, Crabtree Lane,
Fulham, London SW6 6LU, UK.
Telephone 071 381 6007 Fax 071 381 3930

ISBN 1-870-870-344

Printed & bound in Great Britain by
BPCC Paperbacks Ltd, Tring Road, Aylesbury, Bucks, HP20 1LB.

Acknowledgments

With special thanks to UPS Translations, 264 Pentonville Road, London N1 9JY
☎ (071) 837 8300 without whose help this book would have been called "How To
Say 'Please May I have A Beer' In French", and to everybody who contributed in
some way towards the realisation of this very sick idea.

To Martin the Rotweiller -
the Financial Director from Hell

HOW TO SAY FUCK

CONTENTS

OFF IN 50 LANGUAGES

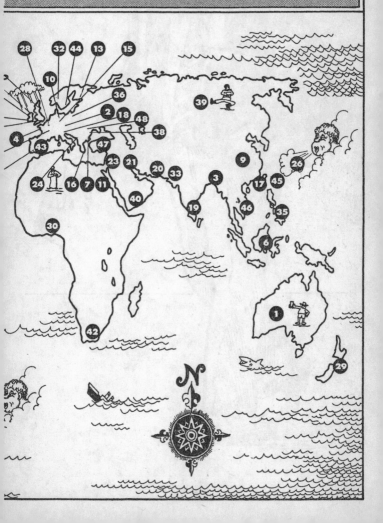

Author's Introduction

It doesn't matter where you go in the world, there's always somebody who won't take 'no' for an answer. It might a Spanish timeshare rep waving a free bottle of bubbly, a toothless beach vendor in Thailand who seems intent on blocking out the sun until you agree to buy something, or perhaps a surly French waiter expecting to receive a first class tip after serving you a second rate meal in a third rate hotel restaurant. They are all out there somewhere, just waiting to annoy, hassle, harangue, cajole, plead and pester.

So what can you do? It's all very well speaking a foreign language well enough to say "no thank you, I'm not terribly interested in purchasing your expertly carved souvenir". Even if you raise your voice and talk to them in slow clearly enunciated English there is still no guarantee that they will get the message. Quite frankly there are times when you are left with only one option: you take a deep breath, look your adversary straight in the eye and tell them to FUCK OFF! in a dialect that you know they will be able to understand. The term 'fuck off' is hard, vicious, rude, direct and definitely not the reply of a potential customer. And that, in a nutshell, is what first inspired me to set about the task of compiling this unique volume.

No Ordinary Phrasebook

Make no mistake *How To Say Fuck Off In 50 Languages* is more than just another phrasebook. It also aims to provide the reader with a wealth of invaluable back-ground material relating to each of our 50 featured destinations.

Did you know, for example, that the average life expectancy in Nigeria is just 48 years? Or that the capital city of Brunei is called Bandar Seri Begawan? Did it ever occur to you that in Taiwan the Pelican bird is regarded as an omen of good luck? Or that the typical stool volume of a healthy Greek adult is an incredible 13 ounces?

These are just a few of the rare and fascinating insights that you will find packed between the pages of this handy, pocket-sized paperback.

Who Am I?

My name is Kelvin Birdseye and I'm a salesman. For my sins, they call me 'The Great White Shark of Premium Products'. Selling is my life. Over the past 20 years or so I've spent more time than I'd care to remember at 35,000 feet above sea level wedged into an aircraft seat in the business section of a jumbo jet. In all I've visited 785 cities in 67 countries; flown on 55 airlines; stayed in 375 hotels and claimed over £3,000,000 in expenses!

By any standards, I like to think of myself as a bit of a high flyer. If you will, a fully paid up citizen of the New Global Village.

So how, you might wonder, did a guy like me get to become an expert on worldwide abuse? Simple, I always carried a pen and notebook. Consequently whenever I had reason to believe that I was being told to 'Fuck Off' by a foreigner, I just asked them to write it down for me. This gave me both the spelling and the pronunciation that I needed - as well as the excuse to shout it right back at them!

This Charming Man

I'm a people person. I've had to learn how to deal with people from all walks of life regardless of age, sex, race or religion. It makes no difference to me whether you're a 'naughty novelty' key-ring carver from Nepal or a Welsh water-colourist who churns out 'cute kitten' kitchen clocks - I like to think that if it ever became necessary I could probably charm the knickers off a nun!

My tongue is my tool and with a few moist flicks I have been known to turn the most unpromising prospect into cold hard commission. It's pure God-given instinct. The Midas Touch of the consummate sales professional. I call it "communicability".

But don't get me wrong, Kelvin Birdseye is more than just an international super-salesman, he's also a creature of intellect: part-time writer, part-time artist, part-time poet and full-time observer of the human condition.

More About Me

Be honest, you can't expect success to be handed to you on a plate - you've got to get out there and graft. I remember my first trip to the Far East. It was back in 1975 and I had flown out to Singapore to negotiate an exclusive manufacturing deal (worth 75K) with Walter Yee, the 25-stone, chain-smoking chairman of XYZ (Hong Kong) Ltd. He was reckoned to be something of a big fish in the world of metal processing, but he evidently didn't realise that he was about to go swimming with the man destined to become known as 'The Great White Shark of Premium Products'. Quite frankly Yee was soon way out of his depth. He had the nerve to suggest that we use low-grade steel to construct my limited edition range of *Sayonara Mr Lawrence* souvenir samurai swords. "D'Jew Let Lo Mo" (Fuck your old mother) I said "just stamp them out of an old tin sheet, no-one will ever notice the difference". And thus my career was forged, so to speak.

But What About You?

You travel the world. You're going places (in more ways than one!). You're cosmopolitan, you're metropolitan, you may even be Neapolitan - but you're damned if you're going to be licked!

Naturally you'll be bright, gifted, popular and attractive. A key decision maker perhaps? But sometimes your exotic fast-moving lifestyle can be brought to a grinding halt by the lumbering intervention of a thoughtless foreigner. Your sap rises, your blood boils and you spit your dummy!

I've had occasion to spit my dummy in more foreign countries than you could shake a stick at, but I've taken the trouble to learn how to deal with it in the local lingo. And now you can do the same! It has to be crude, it has to be colloquial and it has to be right first time. No cock-ups and no dribbling!

To Summarise: A Summary

I've said it before and no doubt I'll say it again: this book is totally unique. This, believe it nor not, is the book that was rejected by over 200 of the world's top publishing houses. Quite frankly, none of them had either the vision or the balls for a project of this magnitude. And I hope they all rot in hell! But slowly.

So welcome, gentle citizen, to the glamourous world of Kelvin Birdseye. But hang onto your hats: it's a world of fast cars, beautiful women, first class hotels, club class travel, shiny suits, glitzy ballgowns, soft furnishings, hard bargaining, big tips, small royalties, company credit cards, cheap cigars, loose ladies, lingering lunches and lost luggage . . . Need I say more?

But let's face it, sometimes the world can be a tough place to work in. That's why I've also tried to include a slice or two of hard-headed commercial street savvy direct from the Birdseye Business Briefcase! And hey, don't knock it till you've tried it!

This then is the ultimate international handbook - the only handbook which contains probably the most important foreign phrase that you'll ever need to know.

Welcome, my friends, to *How To Say Fuck Off In 50 Languages*. Enjoy.

Kelvin Birdseye

September 1993
Brentwood, Essex
(England)

"They say that Australians are basically a bunch of sexist, loud-mouthed drunks, but I once met a group near Wagga Wagga in the Northern Territories who were the complete opposite. Not only were they quiet and reserved, but they also happened to be vegetarian tee-totallers. I am only sorry that they hopped away into the bush before I had a chance to speak to them."

AUSTRALIA

STATUS: COMMONWEALTH NATION **AREA:** 7,682,300 SQ KM (2,965,370 SQ MILES) **POPULATION:** 17,048,347 **CAPITAL CITY:** CANBERRA **LANUGAGE:** AUSTRALIAN **CURRENCY:** AUSTRALIAN DOLLAR **AVERAGE WEEKLY WAGE:** £222.05 **AVERAGE LIFE EXPECTANCY:** 73 YEARS 18 DAYS **FAVOURITE COLOUR:** RED **KEY CITIZENS:** RUPERT MURDOCH, KYLIE MINOGUE **LUCKY NUMBER:** 66 (CLICKETY CLICK) **TYPICAL NUMBER OF BRAIN CELLS:** 65

HOW TO SAY FUCK OFF IN AUSTRALIA

Romanized / pronunciation

GARN STICK YA HID UPPA DID BEERS AHRSE

Literal translation

KINDLY INSERT YOUR HEAD IN THE ANUS OF A DEAD BEAR

"Next to Switzerland, Austria is probably the most expensive country on earth. Last time I was there I took a couple of business contacts out for a few lagers and a curry, and the bill came to more than £2,000! Luckily I was able to claim it back on expenses."

AUSTRIA

STATUS: REPUBLIC **AREA:** 83,855 SQ KM (32,270 SQ MILES) **POPULATION:** 7,775,218 **CAPITAL CITY:** VIENNA **LANGUAGE:** GERMAN **CURRENCY:** SCHILLING **AVERAGE WEEKLY WAGE:** £305.13 **AVERAGE LIFE EXPECTANCY:** 72 YEARS (EXACTLY) **FAVOURITE BAND:** ULTRAVOX **KEY CITIZENS:** NICKI LAUDA, WILLIAM TELL **LUCKY NUMBER:** 4 (TOPS) **TYPICAL HOTEL:** SHERATON

HOW TO SAY FUCK OFF IN AUSTRIA

Romanized / pronunciation

HOW - ABB

Literal translation

FUCK OFF

"Generally speaking, Bangladesh is a country best observed from 35,000 feet in the air, whilst travelling at a speed of 540mph. I once spent 3 days camped at Dacca International Airport waiting for my connection to Taipei. Funnily enough, that was when I learned to say 'Fuck off!' in Bengali."

BANGLADESH

STATUS: PEOPLE'S REPUBLIC **AREA:** 143,998 SQ KM (55,598 SQ MILES)
POPULATION: 90,885,260 **CAPITAL CITY:** DACCA **LANGUAGE:** BENGALI
CURRENCY: TAKA **AVERAGE WEEKLY WAGE:** £2.56 **AVERAGE LIFE
EXPECTANCY:** 47 YEARS **KEY BEVERAGE:** TEA **FAVOURITE COLOUR:** DARK
BLUE **LUCKY NUMBER:** 76 (TROMBONES) **TYPICAL MEAL:** CURRY

HOW TO SAY FUCK OFF IN BANGLADESH

Romanized / pronunciation

JELDI - JOW

Literal translation

FUCK OFF

"Next time you go to Belgium, lay down in a darkened room and let your mind wander over everything that's good about the place: the chocolates, the pastries, the picturesque towns and charming villages... It won't change anything, of course, but it helps to pass the time."

BELGIUM

STATUS: KINGDOM **AREA:** 30,530 SQ KM (11,780 SQ MILES) **POPULATION:** 9,999,999 **CAPITAL CITY:** BRUSSELS **LANGUAGE:** FLEMISH **CURRENCY:** BELGIAN FRANC **AVERAGE WEEKLY WAGE:** £289.74 **AVERAGE LIFE EXPECTANCY:** 72 YEARS **KEY CITIZENS:** PLASTIC BERTRAND, RON ATKINSON **FAVOURITE COLOUR:** BEIGE **LUCKY NUMBER:** 2 (UNLIMITED) **TYPICAL PROFESSION:** BANKER

HOW TO SAY FUCK OFF IN BELGIUM

Romanized / pronunciation

DAH CRUMP IN YAH KLOTEN EN AIN ARM TAH KIRST OM TAH SCHTARTEN

Literal translation

I HOPE YOU GET ITCHY BALLS AND YOUR ARMS ARE TOO SHORT TO SCRATCH THEM

"They say there's an awful lot of coffee in Brazil.
Tell that to the night manager of the SuperContinental
Hotel in Rio. I tried for almost 3 hours to order a cup
of coffee, and a ham sandwich, only to be informed
that in my allegedly drunken state I had dialled the
all-nite launderette by mistake."

BRAZIL

STATUS: FEDERATIVE REPUBLIC **AREA:** 8,511,965 SQ KM (3,285,620 SQ MILES) **POPULATION:** 145,317,282 **CAPITAL CITY:** BRASILIA **LANGUAGE:** PORTUGUESE **CURRENCY:** CRUZADO **AVERAGE WEEKLY WAGE:** £31.61 **AVERAGE LIFE EXPECTANCY:** 62 YEARS **KEY CITIZENS:** PELE, ZICO **FAVOURITE COLOUR:** COFFEE **LUCKY NUMBER:** 13 (UNLUCKY FOR SOME) **TYPICAL GLAND:** THYROID

HOW TO SAY FUCK OFF IN BRAZIL

Romanized / pronunciation

VY COMAR NO COO

Literal translation

TAKE IT IN THE BUM

"The Sultan of Brunei may well be the richest man in the world, but did you know that he is also the world's number one Barry Manilow fan? Apparently the S.O.B. once forked out more than £100,000 to get Barry specially flown in from Detroit in order to serenade his favourite wife, Mandy, on the occasion of her 40th birthday."

BRUNEI

STATUS: SULTANATE **AREA:** 5765 SQ KM (2225 SQ MILES) **POPULATION:** 241,023 **CAPITAL CITY:** BANDAR SERI BEGAWAN **LANGUAGE:** MALAY **CURRENCY:** BRUNEI DOLLAR **AVERAGE WEEKLY WAGE:** £287.16 **AVERAGE LIFE EXPECTANCY:** 60 YEARS **KEY CITIZENS:** THE SULTAN, BARRY MANILOW **FAVOURITE COLOUR:** GOLD **LUCKY NUMBER:** 17 (BILLION DOLLARS) **TYPICAL CLIMATE:** HOT AND HUMID

HOW TO SAY FUCK OFF IN BRUNEI

Romanized / pronunciation

POOKEE MEK ENGCA

Literal translation

FUCK YOUR MOTHER

"A word to the wise: don't get involved in an arm-wrestling contest with a Bulgarian. Though visually unimpressive, they tend to be tough little fellows with the killer instinct of a 50-year-old Sales Director working to a 30 minute deadline. Another piece of advice: don't get yourself hospitalised in Bulgaria!"

BULGARIA

STATUS: PEOPLE'S REPUBLIC **AREA:** 110,910 SQ KM (42,810 SQ MILES)
POPULATION: 9,000,000 **CAPITAL CITY:** SOFIA **LANGUAGE:** BULGARIAN
CURRENCY: LEV **AVERAGE WEEKLY WAGE:** £13.09 **AVERAGE LIFE
EXPECTANCY:** 72 YEARS **KEY FRAGRANCE:** ONIONS **FAVOURITE COLOUR:**
GREY **LUCKY NUMBER:** 57 (VARIETIES) **TYPICAL AMERICAN TV
DETECTIVE:** COLUMBO

HOW TO SAY FUCK OFF IN BULGARIA

Romanized / pronunciation

RAZ - CARAH I YEESEH

Literal translation

FUCK OFF

"Q: How do you fill in the time between appointments on a typically tedious business trip to Vancouver? A: Using only a telephone, a local telephone directory and a litre bottle of vodka I once managed to make contact with 87 men (and 5 women) called Bryan Adams. I told them all to 'Fuck off'!"

CANADA

STATUS: DOMINION **AREA:** 9,922,385 SQ KM (3,830,840 SQ MILES)
POPULATION: 26,028,001 **CAPITAL CITY:** OTTOWA **LANGUAGE:** INUIT
(ESKIMO) **CURRENCY:** CANADIAN DOLLAR **AVERAGE WEEKLY WAGE:**
£278.33 **AVERAGE LIFE EXPECTANCY:** 74 YEARS **KEY CITIZENS:** N/A
FAVOURITE GOLF PROFESSIONAL: NICK FALDO **TYPICAL MEAL:** LUNCH

HOW TO SAY FUCK OFF IN CANADA

Romanized / pronunciation

PREET

Literal translation

FUCK OFF

27

"The Chinese have a reputation for eating virtually anything that has 2 wings or 4 legs (as long as it's not an aeroplane or a table!). Personally speaking, the most peculiar Chinese meal I ever ate was at a Pizza House in Shanghai. If that small round black thing was an olive, then I'm a Chinaman!"

CHINA

STATUS: PEOPLE'S REPUBLIC **AREA:** 9,597,000 SQ KM (3,704,440 SQ MILES) **POPULATION:** 1,195,080,365 **CAPITAL CITY:** BEIJING **LANGUAGE:** MANDARIN (MOSTLY) **CURRENCY:** YUAN **AVERAGE WEEKLY WAGE:** £5.11 **AVERAGE LIFE EXPECTANCY:** 70 YEARS **KEY CITIZENS:** TOO NUMEROUS TO MENTION **FAVOURITE COLOUR:** CUSTARD YELLOW **LUCKY NUMBER:** 96 (TEARS) **TYPICAL SURNAME:** NG

HOW TO SAY FUCK OFF IN CHINA

Romanized / pronunciation

CHOO - EE NEE - DEH

Literal translation

HOLD YOUR ARSE

"If Danish beer is supposed to be the best in the world, I'd like to know why you always feel like shit after drinking 23 pints of the stuff! And another thing, if they're really as liberal and tolerant and laid back as they like to think they are, why do they always make such a fuss about it when you sleep with their wives?"

DENMARK

STATUS: KINGDOM **AREA:** 43,075 SQ KM (16,625 SQ MILES) **POPULATION:** 5,133,000 **CAPITAL CITY:** COPENHAGEN **LANGUAGE:** DANISH **CURRENCY:** DANISH KRONE **AVERAGE WEEKLY WAGE:**£361.53 **AVERAGE LIFE EXPECTANCY:** 74 YEARS 3 DAYS **KEY CITIZENS:** NINA & FREDERICK **FAVOURITE COLOUR:** PINK **LUCKY NUMBER:** 4 (JUST MEN) **TYPICAL RELIGION:** LUTHERAN

HOW TO SAY FUCK OFF IN DENMARK

Romanized / pronunciation

SKREELEH

Literal translation

WALK AWAY

"Until I came to Egypt I honestly didn't think
there was a great deal that anyone could teach 'The
Great White Shark of Premium Products' about the
concept of Pyramid selling. Apparently, I was wrong.
Incidentally, does anyone want to buy 25 gross of
'Lucky Pharaoh' scarab necklaces?
Or a second-hand pyramid?"

EGYPT

STATUS: ARAB REPUBLIC **AREA:** 1,000,250 SQ KM (386,095 SQ MILES)
POPULATION: 52,105,255 **CAPITAL CITY:** CAIRO **LANGUAGE:** ARABIC
CURRENCY: EGYPTIAN POUND **AVERAGE WEEKLY WAGE:** £9.63 **AVERAGE
LIFE EXPECTANCY:** 44 YEARS **KEY PYRAMID:** CHEOPS **FAVOURITE COLOUR:**
SHIT BROWN **LUCKY MEAL:** CHEESE WHOPPER **TYPICAL EXPORT
CROP:** COTTON

HOW TO SAY FUCK OFF IN EGYPT

Romanized / pronunciation

EMSHI - YAY HORRA

Literal translation

GO AWAY DONKEY

"In England's green and pleasant land the world 'fuck' can be used as a verb, a noun, an adjective – and just about any form of punctuation you fucking like (see page 112). Purists of the English language might argue that this denotes a lack of vocabulary, intellect or sensitivity. But then, you can always tell the bastard to 'Fuck off'!"

ENGLAND

STATUS: CONSTITUENT COUNTRY OF THE UNITED KINGDOM **AREA:** 130,360 SQ KM (50,320 SQ MILES) **POPULATION:** 47,885,207 **CAPITAL CITY:** LONDON **CURRENCY:** POUND STERLING **AVERAGE WEEKLY WAGE:** £221.79 **AVERAGE LIFE EXPECTANCY:** 73 YEARS **KEY CITIZENS:** PRINCESS DIANA, DAVE BASSETT **FAVOURITE DAY OF THE WEEK:** TUESDAY **LUCKY NUMBER PLATE:** J577 DJD **TYPICAL VEGETABLE:** JOHN MAJOR

HOW TO SAY FUCK OFF IN ENGLAND

Romanized / pronunciation

FUCK OFF

Literal translation

FUCK OFF

"Finland? Dull dull dull! Megadull! Dullsville, Arizona, in fact! But there's a great 24-hour bar in Kofka called 'Oggi, Oggi, Oggi' where they practice the ancient Finnish art of dwarf-tossing. This isn't quite as disgusting and degrading as you might imagine – potential 'tossers' are supplied with protective rubber gloves and you don't have to swallow it if you don't want to!"

FINLAND

STATUS: REPUBLIC **AREA:** 337,030 SQ KM (130,095 SQ MILES)
POPULATION: 4,967,222 **CAPITAL CITY:** HELSINKI **LANGUAGE:** FINNISH
CURRENCY: MARKKA **AVERAGE WEEKLY WAGE:** £269.23 **AVERAGE LIFE
EXPECTANCY:** 72 YEARS **KEY CITIZENS:** N/A **FAVOURITE SPEILBERG MOVIE:**
JAWS **LUCKY NUMBER:** 16 (MEN ON A DEAD MAN'S CHEST) **TYPICAL
NUMBER OF PINTS OF BEER PER NIGHT:** 16

HOW TO SAY FUCK OFF IN FINLAND

Romanized / pronunciation

PAINOO-VITOON

Literal translation

GO TO CUNT

"According to my mate Jean-Pierre, the French have recently developed the ultimate 'green' vehicle. The so-called 'Garli-car' features a methane driven engine which is powered simply by breathing into a narrow rubber tube connected to the fuel tank. Initial tests indicate that a single belch from a freshly-fed Frenchman can drive the car an amazing 3.2 kilometres at speeds of up to 40mph."

FRANCE

STATUS: REPUBLIC **AREA:** 547,026 SQ KM (211,208 SQ MILES)
POPULATION: 55,623,220 **CAPITAL CITY:** PARIS **LANGUAGE:** FRENCH
CURRENCY: FRENCH FRANC **AVERAGE WEEKLY WAGE:** £306.41 **AVERAGE
LIFE EXPECTANCY:** 73 YEARS (UNFORTUNATELY) **KEY CITIZENS:** VANESSA
PARADIS, MICHEL PLATINI **FAVOURITE SMELL:** FISHY **LUCKY NUMBER:** 7
(SEAS OF RYE) **TYPICAL MEAL:** CHICKEN CHASSEUR

HOW TO SAY FUCK OFF IN FRANCE

Romanized / pronunciation

VAH TOO FAIR FOOTRAH

Literal translation

FUCK OFF

"Be fair. When it comes to food fucking and football,
the Germans are always going to be hard to beat.
Furthermore, they also lead the world in technological
innovation and can hold their booze a lot better than
the Japs. And I'm not just saying that because they
happen to be my most important wholesale customers.
Or am I?"

GERMANY

STATUS: FEDERAL REPUBLIC **AREA:** 356,849 SQ KM (137,740 SQ MILES)
POPULATON: 78,845,222 **CAPITAL CITY:** BERLIN **LANGUAGE:** GERMAN
CURRENCY: DEUTSCHE MARK **AVERAGE WEEKLY WAGE:** £309.23 **AVERAGE**
LIFE EXPECTANCY: 72 YEARS **KEY CITIZENS:** WERNER HERZOG, EVA BRAUN
FAVOURITE MONTH: JANUARY **LUCKY SAUSAGE:** BRATWÜRST **TYPICAL**
ATTENTION SPAN: 1.3 SECONDS

HOW TO SAY FUCK OFF IN GERMANY

Romanized / pronunciation

HOW - ABB

Literal translation

FUCK OFF

"Considering that they're supposed to be one of our most ancient civilisations, you'd have thought that by now the Greeks would have learnt a bit about the preparation of food and wine. Evidently not. In my humble opinion they ought to smash the crockery before rather than after the meal. Then pour a bottle of Metaxa over the kitchen floor and set fire to it."

GREECE

FACT FILE

STATUS: HELLENIC REPUBLIC **AREA:** 131,985 SQ KM (50,945 SQ MILES)
POPULATION: 9,999,998 **CAPITAL CITY:** ATHENS **LANGUAGE:** GREEK
CURRENCY: DRACHMA **AVERAGE WEEKLY WAGE:** £97.43 **AVERAGE LIFE**
EXPECTANCY: 74 YEARS (WOMEN ONLY) **KEY CITIZENS:** ARISTOTLE ONASSIS,
NANA MOUSKUOURI **FAVOURITE AIRLINE:** VIRGIN ATLANTIC **LUCKY**
NUMBER: 50 (WAYS TO LEAVE YOUR LOVER) **TYPICAL STOOL VOLUME:** 13 OZ

HOW TO SAY FUCK OFF IN GREECE

Romanized / pronunciation

MALAKA

Literal translation

WANKER
(IT'S GONE SOFT)

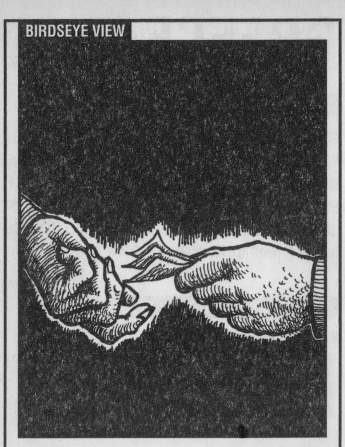

"Hong Kong has always been high on my list of favourite business destinations. It's not just the fact that they do the best fish'n'chips in the Far East (though obviously that's important). It's their instinctive certainty that if you want to get things done there's absolutely no substitute for bribery and corruption."

HONG KONG

STATUS: UK DEPENDENT TERRITORY **AREA:** 1,067 SQ KM (412 SQ MILES)
POPULATION: 5,687,245 **CAPITAL CITY:** VICTORIA **LANGUAGE:** CANTONESE
CURRENCY: HONG KONG DOLLARS **AVERAGE WEEKLY WAGE:** £241.02
AVERAGE LIFE EXPECTANCY: 70 YEARS **KEY CITIZENS:** STEPHEN LI, JOYCE
YIP **FAVOURITE WINGED INSECT:** GRASSHOPPER **LUCKY NUMBER:** 3 (WISE
MEN) **TYPICAL SHOE SIZE:** 7 (MALE) 4.5 (FEMALE)

HOW TO SAY FUCK OFF IN HONG KONG

Romanized / pronunciation

D'JEW LET LO MO

Literal translation

FUCK YOUR OLD MOTHER

THE SNORTING HUSSAR.

"I've always regarded Hungary as the most progressive nation in Eastern Europe. They have been quick to embrace the four basic pillars of western civilisation: hard porn, hamburgers, cocaine and cola. Now I plan to introduce them to the concept of premium quality, limited edition keepsakes and name brand 'Hungarian Heritage Commemorative Pottery'. Watch this space!"

HUNGARY

STATUS: REPUBLIC **AREA:** 93,030 SQ KM (35,910 SQ MILES) **POPULATION:**
10,923,667 **CAPITAL CITY:** BUDAPEST **LANGUAGE:** HUNGARIAN
CURRENCY: FORINT **AVERAGE WEEKLY WAGE:** £49.94 **AVERAGE LIFE**
EXPECTANCY: 70 YEARS **KEY CITIZENS:** TARAS BULBA, EGON RONAY
FAVOURITE COLOUR: DEEP MAROON **LUCKY NUMBER:** 18 (WITH A BULLET)
TYPICAL CAR: FORD GOULASH 1.6i

HOW TO SAY FUCK OFF IN HUNGARY

Romanized / pronunciation

MENJAH FENEHBEH

Literal translation

GO TO HELL

"When it comes to bureaucracy, the Indians are definitely in a class of their own. It once took me nearly 15 minutes to fill out the relevant paperwork entitling me to order a large gin and tonic from a hotel bar in Bombay! Seriously though, when in India always carry a portable fan and a good supply of biros. And be sure to wear loose-fitting clothes."

INDIA

STATUS: REPUBLIC **AREA:** 3,166,830 SQ KM (1,222,395 SQ MILES)
POPULATION: 832,287,343 **CAPITAL CITY:** NEW DELHI **LANGUAGE:** HINDI
CURRENCY: INDIAN RUPEE **AVERAGE WEEKLY WAGE:** £3.45 **AVERAGE LIFE
EXPECTANCY:** 54 YEARS **KEY BODYWEIGHT:** 60KG **FAVOURITE MEATLOAF
TRACK:** BAT OUT OF HELL **LUCKY NUMBER:** 3 (MEN AND A BABY) **TYPICAL
LO-FAT SPREAD:** DELIGHT

HOW TO SAY FUCK OFF IN INDIA

Romanized / pronunciation

JOW APKA MOO KALA KARO

Literal translation

GO AND BLACKEN YOUR FACE

"We writers have to be especially diplomatic when dealing with those lovely fundamentalist folk from Iran. Personally though I can't imagine why anyone would want to write about the sorry inhabitants of a dusty old shitheap of a country where the streets are knee-deep in drool and pistachio shells. But hey, no fatwahs, OK?"

IRAN

STATUS: REPUBLIC **AREA:** 1,648,000 SQ KM (636,130 SQ MILES)
POPULATION: 54,000,000 **CAPITAL CITY:** TEHRAN **LANGUAGE:** FARSI
CURRENCY: RIAL **AVERAGE WEEKLY WAGE:** £12.82 **AVERAGE LIFE
EXPECTANCY:** 52 YEARS **KEY CITIZENS:** RON ATKINSON (OBVIOUSLY) BETTY
BOO **FAVOURITE POP STAR:** LULU **LUCKY FABRIC:** HORSEHAIR **TYPICAL
STATE:** BOREDOM

HOW TO SAY FUCK OFF IN IRAN

Romanized / pronunciation

GOBEH-REESHAT

Literal translation

SHIT IN YOUR BEARD

"Most people rightly regard Saddam Hussein as the latest Mad Mullah from the Middle East. But did you know that he is also a world class snooker player? Back in 1983 I saw him defeat Alex Higgins by 10 frames to 3 in the quarter finals of the Baghdad 'Supergun' Classic. Mind you, Higgins looked to be as pissed as a carrot!"

IRAQ

STATUS: REPUBLIC **AREA:** 438,317 SQ KM (169,235 SQ MILES)
POPULATION: 17,014,211 **CAPITAL CITY:** BAGHDAD **LANGUAGE:**
ARABIC/KURDISH **CURRENCY:** IRAQI DINAR **AVERAGE WEEKLY WAGE:**
£12.82 **AVERAGE LIFE EXPECTANCY:** N/A **KEY CITIZENS:** SADDAM HUSSEIN,
MIKE READ (NOT THE DJ) **FAVOURITE AD AGENCY:** YOUNG, GIFTED AND
RUBICAM **LUCKY NUMBER:** 40 (THIEVES) **TYPICAL DAIRY PRODUCT:** MILK

HOW TO SAY FUCK OFF IN IRAQ

Romanized / pronunciation

KOOS-IM-MUK

Literal translation

GO FUCK YOUR MOTHER

"I own a small percentage in a chain of souvenir outlets called 'Yankers Only', which, as you might imagine, is aimed largely at the US tourist market. Next year we hope to introduce three new products to the range: hand-painted porcelain potatoes, bronze'n'pewter pickaxe handles and 'his'n'hers' designer donkey jackets – fashioned out of pure 100% donkey skin!"

IRELAND

STATUS: REPUBLIC **AREA:** 68,895 SQ KM (26,595 SQ MILES) **POPULATION:** 3,552,201 **CAPITAL CITY:** DUBLIN **LANGUAGE:** IRISH **CURRENCY:** PUNT **AVERAGE WEEKLY WAGE:** £188.46 **AVERAGE LIFE EXPECTANCY:** 73 YEARS **KEY CITIZENS:** JOHNNY LOGAN, TERRY WOGAN **FAVOURITE TIME OF DAY:** PUB OPENING TIME **LUCKY PLANT:** SHAMROCK **TYPICAL IQ:** 96

HOW TO SAY FUCK OFF IN IRELAND

Romanized / pronunciation

GO-REV-TOE-CUSH-SEERI-AIR-DE-VOGARLY

Literal translation

MAY YOU HAVE AN ETERNAL ITCH ON YOUR BALLS

"I don't know why it is, but a lot of people seem to think I'm Jewish (maybe it's because I've got a big nose and happen to drive a Volvo!). Anyhow, the trouble with the Israelis is that they eat too much dried herring in their diet. Consequently when they fart it tends to smell rather like a partially decomposed animal."

ISRAEL

STATUS: STATE **AREA:** 20,700 SQ KM (8,015 SQ MILES) **POPULATION:**
4,575,233 **CAPITAL CITY:** JERUSALEM **LANGUAGE:** HEBREW **CURRENCY:**
NEW SHECKEL **AVERAGE WEEKLY WAGE:** £156.93 (WITH OVERTIME)
AVERAGE LIFE EXPECTANCY: 72 YEARS **KEY CITIZENS:** SAM & RACHEL KEY
FAVOURITE SOAP: EASTENDERS **LUCKY NUMBER:**808 (STATE) **TYPICAL
SKIN DISEASE:** ACNE

HOW TO SAY FUCK OFF IN ISRAEL

Romanized / pronunciation

LEK LEHIZ-BAYEN

Literal translation

GO AND FUCK YOURSELF

"I like Italy. I like the food, I like the climate
and I like the scenery. What's more, I like to
do business with Italians. I find them stylish, emotive,
sexy, gregarious and trusting – with an almost childlike
naiveté (which might explain why the stupid bastards
rarely bother to read the small print on
their contracts!)"

ITALY

STATUS: REPUBLIC **AREA:** 301,245 SQ KM (116,280 SQ MILES)
POPULATION: 57473,217 **CAPITAL CITY:** ROME **LANGUAGE:** ITALIAN
CURRENCY: LIRA **AVERAGE WEEKLY WAGE:** £258.97 **AVERAGE LIFE
EXPECTANCY:** 73 YEARS **KEY CITIZENS:** GIORGIO ARMANI, SOPHIA LOREN
FAVOURITE COLOUR: OLIVE GREEN **LUCKY NUMBER:** (FELLINI'S) $8\frac{1}{2}$
TYPICAL FASHION ACCESSORY: SUNGLASSES

HOW TO SAY FUCK OFF IN ITALY

Romanized / pronunciation

VAH FAN-COOLOH

Literal translation

FUCK OFF

"When I'm not working hard I like to play hard (hey, don't knock it till you've tried it!). On a recent pleasure trip to Jamaica I was warned by the hotel witch doctor to 'watch out for Hurricane Leroy'. I assumed that he was talking about a local pool shark or demon fast bowler until the island was suddenly hit by a violent tropical storm with winds gusting up to 120mph."

JAMAICA

STATUS: STATE **AREA:** 11,425 SQ KM (4,410 SQ MILES) **POPULATION:** 2,363,808 **CAPITAL CITY:** KINGSTON **LANGUAGE:** LOCAL PATOIS **CURRENCY** JAMAICAN DOLLAR **AVERAGE WEEKLY WAGE:** £35 **AVERAGE LIFE EXPECTANCY:** 70 YEARS **KEY CITIZENS:** BOB MARLEY, RON ATKINSON **FAVOURITE TROPIC:** CANCER **LUCKY SEAFOOD:** LOBSTER **TYPICAL STARSIGN:** ARIES

HOW TO SAY FUCK OFF IN JAMAICA

Romanized / pronunciation

FOCKOFF
BLODKLAAT

Literal translation

FUCK OFF

"The Japanese are a nation to whom ritual and respect are paramount. As a business visitor you must prepare yourself for the ceremony of the business card. It should be received with a sharp bow of the head, studied closely with an expression of awe then torn into small pieces and placed in the nearest ashtray. Finally you return the compliment by handing your Japanese host a business card that was given to you by the idiot you sat next to on the plane!"

JAPAN

STATUS: IMPERIAL MONARCHY **AREA:** 369,700 SQ KM (142,705 SQ MILES)
POPULATION: 123,000,001 **CAPITAL CITY:** TOKYO **LANGUAGE:** JAPANESE
CURRENCY: YEN **AVERAGE WEEKLY WAGE:** £410.48 **AVERAGE LIFE**
EXPECTANCY: 76 YEARS **KEY CITIZENS:** YOKO ONO, BILL BEAUMONT
FAVOURITE TYPE OF PLASTIC: TUPPERWARE **LUCKY GEMSTONE:** OPAL
TYPICAL GOLF HANDICAP: 36

HOW TO SAY FUCK OFF IN JAPAN

Romanized / pronunciation

EETEH
SHIMAHL

Literal translation

PISS OFF

"I spent my second honeymoon in Acapulco (actually it was my first honeymoon with my second wife but you know what I mean). Anyhow, the first week we were there it rained every day, then we got hit by a minor earthquake, and finally the day before we were due to leave, my bride ran off with the tennis pro from the hotel. I haven't been back there since!"

MEXICO

FACT FILE

STATUS: FEDERAL REPUBLIC **AREA:** 1,972,545 SQ KM (761,400 SQ MILES) **POPULATION:** 83,000,000 **CAPITAL CITY :** MEXICO CITY **LANGUAGE:** SPANISH **CURRENCY:** MEXICAN PESO **AVERAGE WEEKLY WAGE:** £53.66 **AVERAGE LIFE EXPECTANCY:** 65 YEARS **KEY CITIZENS:** PANCHO VILLA, RON ATKINSON **FAVOURITE COLOUR:** MAUVE **LUCKY NUMBER:** (LEGS) 11 **TYPICAL POPULATION DENSITY:** 41.9 PER SQ KM

HOW TO SAY FUCK OFF IN MEXICO

Romanized / pronunciation

VEHTAY A LA CHINGADA

Literal translation

FUCK OFF

"The Dutch are the only people I know who choose to live on or below the sea bed. This is due to the fact that the lazy sods spend most of their time reclining in a horizontal position and therefore become instantly nauseous when exposed to altitudes in excess of 5 metres. Traditionally, they wear little wooden boats on their feet in case the tide comes in unexpectedly."

NETHERLANDS

STATUS: KINGDOM **AREA:** 33,940 SQ KM (13,105 SQ MILES) **POPULATION:** 14,851,010 **CAPITAL CITY:** AMSTERDAM **LANGUAGE:** DUTCH **CURRENCY:** GUILDER **AVERAGE WEEKLY WAGE:** £274.35 **AVERAGE LIFE EXPECTANCY:** 74 **KEY CITIZENS:** FANNY BLANKERS-KOEN **FAVOURITE HEADGEAR:** DUTCH CAP **LUCKY NUMBER:** 3 (DEGREES)

HOW TO SAY FUCK OFF IN THE NETHERLANDS

Romanized / pronunciation

DONDER ROWP

Literal translation

FUCK OFF

"Two hundred and fifty years ago New Zealand was colonised by a bunch of miserable Glaswegians who never really came to terms with the fact that the original inhabitants were a great deal saner, more civilised and better looking than themselves. These days it's populated by a bunch of miserable, rugby-playing sheep-shaggers who seem to be stuck in a 1950s time warp. Personally my favourite spot on the island is the airport departure lounge."

NEW ZEALAND

STATUS: DOMINION **AREA:** 265,150 SQ KM (102,350 SQ MILES)
POPULATION: 3,333,332 **CAPITAL CITY:** WELLINGTON **LANGUAGE:** MAORI
CURRENCY: NEW ZEALAND DOLLAR **AVERAGE WEEKLY WAGE:** £157.69
AVERAGE LIFE EXPECTANCY: 73 YEARS **KEY CITIZENS:** LARRY LAMB, SAM
SHEPHERD **FAVOURITE TYPE OF COAT:** SHEEPSKIN **LUCKY EMBLEM:**
GARFIELD THE AMUSING KIWI BIRD **TYPICAL DAIRY PRODUCT:** BUTTER

HOW TO SAY FUCK OFF IN NEW ZEALAND

Romanized / pronunciation

HIREE - RAH

Literal translation

GO AWAY

"Some years ago I was in Lagos for a senior management convention. After business was concluded the organisers had arranged an afternoon of watersports at the local yacht club. Listen, have you ever tried to water-ski with literally dozens of corpses bobbing round your ankles? I later found out that they were mostly ex-pat Belgian architects."

NIGERIA

STATUS: FEDERAL REPUBLIC **AREA:** 923,850 SQ KM (356,605 SQ MILES)
POPULATION: 101,991,675 **CAPITAL CITY:** LAGOS **LANGUAGE:** HAUSA
(Tribal dialects) **CURRENCY:** NAIRA **AVERAGE WEEKLY WAGE:** £3.86
AVERAGE LIFE EXPECTANCY: 48 YEARS **KEY CITIZENS:** JOHNNY TIGER,
MARJORIE PROOPS **FAVOURITE ARMED FORCE:** THE ARMY **LUCKY GLAND:**
ADRENAL **TYPICAL MEAL:** MEDALLIONS OF BROILED BUFFALO IN A
WALNUT AND BLACKCURRANT SAUCE

HOW TO SAY FUCK OFF IN NIGERIA

Romanized / pronunciation

DAH DOOROO WAHN-GAH

Literal translation

FUCK YOU

"Whilst en-route to a Retail Park in Dungannon,
my car was halted by a group of armed paramilitary
thugs. They accused me of being a 'flash Catholic
bastard' (I bear a passing resemblance to Terry Wogan
and happened to be driving a red Corvette Stingray)
and were threatening to give me a good kicking.
Hey, be honest – do you blame them?"

NORTHERN IRELAND

STATUS: COMPLETELY FUCKED **AREA:** 14,150 SQ KM (5,460 SQ MILES)
POPULATION: 1,601,666 **CAPITAL CITY:** BELFAST **LANGUAGE:** NORTHERN
IRISH **CURRENCY:** POUND STERLING **AVERAGE WEEKLY WAGE;** £180.28
AVERAGE LIFE EXPECTANCY: N/A **KEY CITIZENS:** IAN PAISLEY, BARRY
MCGUIGAN **FAVOURITE COLOUR:** ORANGE **LUCKY MEAT:** MUTTON **TYPICAL
BLOOD PRESSURE READING:** 160/80

HOW TO SAY FUCK OFF IN NORTHERN IRELAND

Romanized / pronunciation

FUCKOFFITEOVIT

Literal translation

PLEASE GO AWAY

"Are you an animal lover? Then maybe you've heard of 'Pet-o-Vibe' – the vibrating pet bed that's guaranteed to keep your pooch permanently in the pink. If so, it might interest you to know that they are partially manufactured from lumps of prime Norwegian whale blubber. This fine and versatile material can also be used to construct Spacehoppers (remember them?), Bouncy Castles and Shell Suits."

NORWAY

STATUS: KINGDOM **AREA:** 323,895 SQ KM (125,025 SQ MILES) **POPULATION:** 4,197,999 **CAPITAL CITY:** OSLO **LANGUAGE:** NORWEGIAN **CURRENCY:** NORWEGIAN KRONE **AVERAGE WEEKLY WAGE:** £361.53 **AVERAGE LIFE EXPECTANCY:** 75 YEARS **KEY CITIZENS:** EDUARD MUNCH, RON ATKINSON **FAVOURITE CARTOON CHARACTER:** POPEYE **LUCKY NUMBER:** 7 (ROOMS OF GLOOM) **TYPICAL BREAKFAST SNACK:** PICKLED HERRING

HOW TO SAY FUCK OFF IN NORWAY

Romanized / pronunciation

DRAH TILL HELL-VETAH

Literal translation

GO TO HELL

"As a 'frequent flyer' I get to meet some interesting people. A few years ago on a flight from London to Karachi I sat next to a young chap called Jimmy Khan. In those days he was just a budding rag-trade entrepreneur, and I flatter myself that during the 8-hour trip I was able to pass on some pretty significant marketing wisdom. Subsequently, in 1987, he launched the 'Mainly Moslems' chain of ethnic boutiques followed a year later by the first 'Turbans'R'Us' warehouse. The rest, as they say, is history."

PAKISTAN

STATUS: ISLAMIC REPUBLIC **AREA:** 803,943 SQ KM (310,404 SQ MILES)
POPULATION: 105,799,467 **CAPITAL CITY:** KARACHI **LANGUAGE:** URDU
CURRENCY: PAKISTANI RUPEE **AVERAGE WEEKLY WAGE:** £5.51 **AVERAGE
LIFE EXPECTANCY:** 52 YEARS **KEY CITIZENS:** IMRAN KHAN, KUBLA KHAN
FAVOURITE TV SPORT: HOCKEY **LUCKY NUMBER:** 22 (ALL THE 2'S)
TYPICAL METHOD OF TRAVEL: BICYCLE

HOW TO SAY FUCK OFF IN PAKISTAN

Romanized / pronunciation

MANG-KEE

Literal translation

FUCK OFF

"Lake Titicaca, the Andes mountain range, the ancient city of Lima... Peru is like nowhere else on earth. It's also in a class of its own when it comes to serving up pedigree canine cuisine. Where else could you find such delicacies on the menu as stuffed Pekinese with peppercorn or char-broiled fillets of prime Oxfordshire Spaniel?"

PERU

STATUS: REPUBLIC **AREA:** 1,285,215 SQ KM (496,095 SQ MILES)
POPULATION: 21,505,777 **CAPITAL CITY:** LIMA **LANGUAGE:** QUECHUA
CURRENCY: INTI **AVERAGE WEEKLY WAGE:** £20 **AVERAGE LIFE EXPECTANCY:**
57 YEARS **KEY CITIZENS:** MICK JAGGER, DES TUTU **FAVOURITE
PUNCTUATION MARK / INTESTINE:** THE COLON **LUCKY NUMBER:** 21 (KEY OF
THE DOOR) **TYPICAL PARTY ANIMAL:** THE LLAMA FROM LIMA

HOW TO SAY FUCK OFF IN PERU

Romanized / pronunciation

ANDATAY AL AH MIERR-AH

Literal translation

GO TO SHIT

"These days you have to be extra careful who you pick up in a bar or night-club. This is especially true in the Far East: I remember one time I was drinking at the Purple Pussycat in Manila when this gorgeous looking creature that I'd had my eye on for most of the evening sat down at the table opposite, took out a pipe, farted loudly and began to talk about football in a deep voice."

PHILIPPINES

STATUS: REPUBLIC **AREA:** 300,000 SQ KM (115,800 SQ MILES)
POPULATION: 58,930,444 **CAPITAL CITY:** MANILA **LANGUAGE:** PILIPINO
(TAGALOG) **CURRENCY:** PILLIPINE PESO **AVERAGE WEEKLY WAGE:** £10.55
AVERAGE LIFE EXPECTANCY: 62 YEARS **KEY CITIZENS:** IMELDA MARCOS,
RON ATKINSON **FAVOURITE COMPUTER GAME:** SUPERMARIO BROS II
LUCKY HAIRSTYLE: PONYTAIL **TYPICAL INDOOR REPTILE:** LIZARD

HOW TO SAY FUCK OFF IN THE PHILIPPINES

Romanized / pronunciation

OOMAH-LEES KAH DEE YAHN

Literal translation

PUSH OFF

"Apparently geneticists have discovered that Pope
Paul III has a DNA molecular structure similar to the
South American Anteater and that the symbolic
ground kissing for which he has become famous is
actually no more than an instinctive food foraging
impulse. It's amazing what you can learn from the
back of a beermat."

POLAND

STATUS: REPUBLIC **AREA:** 312,685 SQ KM (120,675 SQ MILES)
POPULATION: 37,812,000 **CAPITAL CITY:** WARSAW **LANGUAGE:** POLISH
CURRENCY: ZLOTY **AVERAGE WEEKLY WAGE:** £21.28 **AVERAGE LIFE**
EXPECTANCY: 71 YEARS **KEY CITIZENS:** POPE JOHN PAUL II, LECH WALESA
FAVOURITE OLYMPIC SPORT: POLE VAULT **LUCKY PEPPERMINT:** POLO
TYPICAL SHOE-CLEANING AGENT: POLISH

HOW TO SAY FUCK OFF IN POLAND

Romanized / pronunciation

ODD
PLEPERSH - YEH

Literal translation

PEPPER OFF

"A recent survey into European sexual
practices by the popular UK women's magazine
'Off Games' claimed that a staggering
(and I do mean staggering!) 38% of Portuguese
women voluntarily performed anal intercourse.
Presumably the other 62% had it
thrust upon them!"

PORTUGAL

STATUS: REPUBLIC **AREA:** 91,630 SQ KM (35,370 SQ MILES) **POPULATION:** 10,548,784 **CAPITAL CITY:** LISBON **LANGUAGE:** PORTUGUESE **CURRENCY:** ESCUDO **AVERAGE WEEKLY WAGE:** £30.76 **AVERAGE LIFE EXPECTANCY:** 69 YEARS **KEY CITIZENS:** CHRISTOPHER COLUMBUS, DEAN SAUNDERS **FAVOURITE BAND:** BLACK LACE **LUCKY NUMBER:** 7 (DEADLY SINS) **TYPICAL REACTION:** BEWILDERMENT

HOW TO SAY FUCK OFF IN PORTUGAL

Romanized / pronunciation

VY COMAR NO COO

Literal translation

TAKE IT IN THE BUM

"Once upon a time in a restaurant in Romania, I teamed up with an ex-Olympic gymnast called Irena. Following a crazy night of caviar and vodka she drove us both back to her Bucharest boudoir – in a two-tone Lada. There, after a few basic floor exercises, (and another bottle of vodka) we attempted what can only be described as a triple Sukohara with full-twisting dismount. I awarded her 9.975."

ROMANIA

STATUS: REPUBLIC **AREA:** 237,501 SQ KM (91,675 SQ MILES) **POPULATION:** 23,047,474 **CAPITAL CITY:** BUCHAREST **LANGUAGE:** ROMANIAN **CURRENCY:** LEU **AVERAGE WEEKLY WAGE:** £8.71 **AVERAGE LIFE EXPECTANCY:** 70 YEARS **KEY CITIZENS:** N/A **FAVOURITE SCREEN ADAPTATION OF AN ANDREW LLOYD WEBBER MUSICAL:** EVITA **TYPICAL ROMANIAN VAMPIRE:** COUNT DRACULA

HOW TO SAY FUCK OFF IN ROMANIA

Romanized / pronunciation

DOOTY EEN PEESH-DAH

Literal translation

GO BACK TO YOUR MOTHER'S CUNT

"There have been rumours that Andrei Androvnich, the Super heavyweight weightlifter and 1980 Olympic champion, is in fact a Siberian Brown Bear. Androvnich was apparently shaved before receiving plastic surgery to his hands and face. When reporters tried to contact him to substantiate the claim, they were told by his wife Yogi that he was taking a nap and wouldn't be available until the Spring."

RUSSIA

FACT FILE

STATUS: QUO **AREA:** 17,078,004 SQ KM (6,592,110 SQ MILES)
POPULATION: 148,214,036 **CAPITAL CITY:** MOSCOW **LANGUAGE:** RUSSIAN
CURRENCY: ROUBLES **AVERAGE WEEKLY WAGE:** £11.91 **AVERAGE LIFE**
EXPECTANCY: 70 YEARS **KEY CITIZENS:** BORIS YELTSIN, WHITNEY
HOUSTON **FAVOURITE COLOUR:** WHITE **LUCKY NUMBER:** 7 (BRIDES FOR
SEVEN BROTHERS) **TYPICAL DRINK:** VODKA

HOW TO SAY FUCK OFF IN RUSSIA

Romanized / pronunciation

OT-YEH-BEES

Literal translation

PISS OFF

"In his best-selling hardback 'Sex In The Sand', the noted German anthropologist Herman Bratwürst contends that 80% of Arab males enjoy wearing long dresses with stockings and suspenders. Even more surprisingly, over half of those he interviewed said they wished they were Scottish so that they could wear the shorter, sexier kilt."

SAUDI ARABIA

STATUS: KINGDOM **AREA:** 2,149,690 SQ KM (830,000 SQ MILES)
POPULATION: 11,947,863 **CAPITAL CITY:** RIYADH **LANGUAGE:** ARABIC
CURRENCY: RIYAL **AVERAGE WEEKLY WAGE:** £95.67 **AVERAGE LIFE**
EXPECTANCY: 53 YEARS **KEY CITIZENS:** RON ATKINSON, ALVIN STARDUST
FAVOURITE NUMBER OF HANDS: 2 **LUCKY NUMBER OF HANDS:** 2 **TYPICAL**
NUMBER OF HANDS: 1.7

HOW TO SAY FUCK OFF IN SAUDI ARABIA

Romanized / pronunciation

EEB-N AL CALB

Literal translation

SON OF A DOG

"I'm a people person, but I'm afraid that I have to draw the line when it comes to the Scots. I find them aggressive, rude, belligerent and liable to throw up their lunch at any given moment. That's why we employ no less than six of them in our credit control department!"

SCOTLAND

FACT FILE

STATUS: UK CONSTITUENT COUNTRY **AREA:** 78,750 SQ KM (30,400 SQ MILES) **POPULATION:** 5,098,160 **CAPITAL CITY:** EDINBURGH **LANGUAGE:** GIBBERISH **CURRENCY:** POOND STERLING **AVERAGE WEEKLY WAGE:** £177.28 **AVERAGE LIFE EXPECTANCY:** 65 YEARS **KEY CITIZENS:** JOCK WALLACE, SHEENA EASTON **FAVOURITE TYPE OF BOOZE:** WHUSKY **LUCKY NUMBER:** 100 (PIPERS) **TYPICAL PENILE DIMENSION:** 2¾ INCHES (WHEN FULLY ERECT)

HOW TO SAY FUCK OFF IN SCOTLAND

Romanized / pronunciation

GA'YAFUGGINBAZZA!

Literal translation

GET OUT OF IT YOU FUCKING BASTARD

"South Africa is a place where, with a bit of hard graft and a lot of luck, even the most worthless individual has a chance to drag themselves out of the gutter and become a multi-millionaire businessman. Unless, of course, they happen to be black."

SOUTH AFRICA

STATUS: REPUBLIC **AREA:** 1,184,825 SQ KM (457,345 SQ MILES)
POPULATION: 30,000,000 **CAPITAL CITY:** PRETORIA/CAPE TOWN
LANGUAGE: AFRIKAANS **CURRENCY:** RAND **AVERAGE WEEKLY WAGE:**
£42.46 **AVERAGE LIFE EXPECTANCY:** 60 YEARS **KEY CITIZENS:** WINNIE
MANDELA, ERIC MORLEY **FAVOURITE COLOUR:** WHITE **LUCKY NUMBER:** 12
(ANGRY MEN) **TYPICAL HOBBY:** GARDENING

HOW TO SAY FUCK OFF IN SOUTH AFRICA

Romanized / pronunciation

FOOTSECK

Literal translation

FUCK OFF

"Why would anyone in their right mind want to go
to a place that sells beer that tastes of piss in order to
meet drunken English girls who smell like fish and
chip shops, and swim shoulder to shoulder in raw
sewage with thousands of complete strangers?
It beats the hell out of me."

SPAIN

STATUS: KINGDOM **AREA:** 504,880 SQ KM (194,885 SQ MILES)
POPULATION: 39,585,237 **CAPITAL CITY:** MADRID **LANGUAGE:** SPANISH
CURRENCY: PESETA **AVERAGE WEEKLY WAGE:** £174.35 **AVERAGE LIFE
EXPECTANCY:** 73 YEARS **KEY CITIZENS:** SEVERIANO BALLESTEROS, SHARON
STONE **FAVOURITE TV SPORT:** NUDE VOLLEYBALL **LUCKY PLUMBER:**
DYNOROD **TYPICAL CHRISTIAN NAMES:** PEDRO (MALE) CONCHITA (FEMALE)

HOW TO SAY FUCK OFF IN SPAIN

Romanized / pronunciation

CAH-GO EN LAH LECH-AY DAY TOO MADRAY

Literal translation

I SHIT IN YOUR MOTHER'S MILK

"They're sexy, they're successful, and, sometimes,
they're simply suicidal. Yes, I'm talking about the
Swedes. What is it about the place that could have
inspired the music of Abba, the tennis of Borg and
Edberg, and the movies of Ingmar Bergman?
I'll tell you what it is: it's the miserable
fucking weather!"

SWEDEN

STATUS: KINGDOM **AREA:** 449,790 SQ KM (173,620 SQ MILES)
POPULATION: 8,500,000 **CAPITAL CITY:** STOCKHOLM **LANGUAGE:** SWEDISH
CURRENCY: SWEDISH KRONA **AVERAGE WEEKLY WAGE:** £379.48 **AVERAGE
LIFE EXPECTANCY:** 75 YEARS **KEY CITIZENS:** DEREK VOLVO, JEAN SAAB
FAVOURITE PASTIME: FISHING **LUCKY INSECT:** FLY **TYPICAL TYPE OF
PASTRY:** FLAKY

HOW TO SAY FUCK OFF IN SWEDEN

Romanized / pronunciation

DRAH DEET PEH-PARRN VEXER

Literal translation

GO WHERE THE PEPPER GROWS

"Do you remember how, when you were a kid, all the cheap, tacky toys you got for your birthday seemed to be made in Hong Kong or Taiwan, whereas sophisticated products like cars, TVs and stereos were manufactured in he UK? Now it's the other way round! At this rate it won't be long before we find ourselves living in mud huts and munching rice and noodles!"

TAIWAN

STATUS: REPUBLIC **AREA:** 35,990 SQ KM (13,890 SQ MILES) **POPULATION:** 19,985,001 **CAPITAL CITY:** TAIPEI **LANGUAGE:** MANDARIN CHINESE **CURRENCY:** NEW TAIWAN DOLLAR **AVERAGE WEEKLY WAGE:** £147.43 **AVERAGE LIFE EXPECTANCY:** 70 YEARS **KEY INGREDIENTS:** RICE AND GARLIC **FAVOURITE CHINESE RESTAURANT:** THE GOLDEN DRAGON IN HOUNSLOW **LUCKY BIRD:** THE PELICAN **TYPICAL STATUS QUO ALBUM:** DOG OF TWO HEAD

HOW TO SAY FUCK OFF IN TAIWAN

Romanized / pronunciation

GAN NEE NYOU

Literal translation

FUCK YOUR MOTHER

"In Thailand you not only have to be careful what you say, you have to be careful how you say it. They speak a tonal language and the same word can have up to five different meanings. I won't tell you where I was or how much I'd had to drink, but I was under the distinct impression that I'd requested the full executive massage with extras, so you can imagine my disappointment when somebody handed me a bag of chicken's feet and a bowl of fried rice!"

THAILAND

STATUS: KINGDOM **AREA:** 514,000 SQ KM (198,405 SQ MILES)
POPULATION: 54,975,420 **CAPITAL CITY:** BANGKOK **LANGUAGE:** THAI
CURRENCY: BAHT **AVERAGE WEEKLY WAGE:** £20.57 **AVERAGE LIFE
EXPECTANCY:** 61 YEARS **KEY CITIZENS:** JAMES WATTANA, KID GALAXY
FAVOURITE BODY PART: THE LEFT SHOULDER **LUCKY NUMBER:** 333 (ALL
THE 3'S) **TYPICAL METHOD OF RICE PREPARATION:** BOILING

HOW TO SAY FUCK OFF IN THAILAND

Romanized / pronunciation

PY HY PON, MEN KEY NAH

Literal translation

BUZZ OFF SHITFACE

"Is it just me, or does everyone think that a doner kebab with thinly sliced lettuce bears a startling resemblance to the female genitalia? And whilst we're on the subject, why does that creamy taramasalata stuff smell like my wife's knickers? They're bloody sex mad, those Turks!"

TURKEY

STATUS: REPUBLIC **AREA:** 779,450 SQ KM (300,870 SQ MILES)
POPULATION: 52,860,404 **CAPITAL CITY:** ANKARA **LANGUAGE:** TURKISH
CURRENCY: TURKISH LIRA **AVERAGE WEEKLY WAGE:** £27.82 **AVERAGE LIFE
EXPECTANCY:** 61 YEARS **KEY CITIZENS:** BERNARD MATTHEWS, RON
ATKINSON **FAVOURITE COLOUR:** CRISPY GOLDEN BROWN **LUCKY NUMBER:**
2 (FAT LADIES) **TYPICAL STUFFING INGREDIENTS:** SAGE AND ONION

HOW TO SAY FUCK OFF IN TURKEY

Romanized / pronunciation

FEEKTEER

Literal translation

FUCK OFF

"Few people would imagine that this God-forsaken place could be a particularly fertile hunting ground for the international super-salesman. Quite frankly, it isn't! I go there to indulge my passion for big ladies with headscarves and designer stubble. Hey, don't knock it till you've tried it!"

UKRAINE

STATUS: REPUBLIC **AREA:** 603,700 SQ KM (233,030 SQ MILES)
POPULATION: 51,604,266 **CAPTAL CITY:** KIEV **LANGUAGE:** UKRANIAN
CURRENCY: ROUBLE **AVERAGE WEEKLY WAGE:** £2.41 **AVERAGE LIFE**
EXPECTANCY: 70 YEARS **KEY CITIZENS:** RON ATKINSON, SERGE BUBKA
FAVOURITE JACKIE COLLINS NOVEL: HOLLYWOOD WIVES **LUCKY NUMBER:**
5 (GOLD RINGS) **TYPICAL SEX POSITION:** 'DOGGIE FASHION'

HOW TO SAY FUCK OFF IN UKRAINE

Romanized / pronunciation

VLDT
SHEP - EES

Literal translation

PISS OFF

"The United States is the world's melting pot.
You'll find any number of micks, spicks, jews, japs,
commies, chinks, krauts, wops, dagos, swedes, slopes,
blacks, polacks, redskins, rednecks and
fundamentalists. So next time you go there, be sure to
take this book (and maybe a bullet-proof vest as well)
because you're sure as hell gonna need them!"

USA

STATUS: FEDERAL REPUBLIC **AREA:** 9,371,786 SQ KM (3,618,467 SQ MILES) **POPULATION:** 246,093,111 **CAPITAL CITY:** WASHINGTON DC **LANGUAGE:** AMERICAN **CURRENCY:** US DOLLAR **AVERAGE WEEKLY WAGE:** £288.71 **AVERAGE LIFE EXPECTANCY:** 73 YEARS **KEY CITIZENS:** LARRY FORTENSKY, MADONNA **FAVOURITE WORD:** ME **LUCKY FABRIC:** DENIM **TYPICAL PRESIDENTIAL CANDIDATE:** WALTER MONDALE

HOW TO SAY FUCK OFF IN THE USA

Romanized / pronunciation

FARKEEW!

Literal translation

FUCK YOU

"Do you remember an odd-looking bloke called Neil
Kinnock? Apparently he used to run something called
the Labour Party. Anyhow, he introduced himself to
yours truly at a Motorway Service Station just outside
Newport and tried to get me interested in some sort of
life insurance plan. I kid you not, the man didn't stop
talking for almost 20 minutes and even then I was
none the wiser! Wales? Quite frankly you can keep it!"

WALES

STATUS: UK PRINCIPALITY **AREA:** 20,760 SQ KM (8,015 SQ MILES) **POPULATION:**
2,863,944 **CAPITAL CITY:** CARDIFF **LANGUAGE:** WELSH **CURRENCY:** POUNDS
STERLING **AVERAGE WEEKLY WAGE:** THIRTY-FIVE POUNDS, SEVENTEEN
SHILLINGS AND TUPPENCE THREE FARTHINGS **KEY CITIZENS:** HARRY SECOMBE,
TOM JONES **FAVOURITE COLOUR:** GRASS GREEN **LUCKY NUMBER:** 177
(HIGHEST 3 DART CHECKOUT) **TYPICAL TIME OF DAY:**
BREAKFAST TIME

HOW TO SAY FUCK OFF IN WALES

Romanized / pronunciation

FUCK OFF BOYO

Literal translation

FUCK OFF

FUCK FUCK FUCK

The word "Fuck" describes many emotions. No other word can be used in such varied grammatical nuances. It can be used as a noun, (I don't give a fuck), as an adjective (It's a fucking beauty), as a verb in its transitive form (The game is fucked by the weather) and the intransitive form (He well and truly fucked it). Here are a few more practical examples:

Denial   *I'll be fucked if I did.*
Perplexity   *I know fuck all about it.*
Apathy   *Who gives a fuck anyway?*
Greeting   *How the fuck are you?*
Goodbye   *Fuck off!*
Resignation   *Oh fuck it!*
Derision   *He fucked everything up.*

Over the years the word has been used by some very famous people, the more notable of these being:

"What the fuck was that?" *Mayor of Hiroshima*
"Who's going to fucking know?" *President Nixon*
"Watch out - he'll have some fucker's eye out!" *King Harold*
"She's just a fucking research assistant" *David Mellor*
"He's just a fucking mate" *Jeremy Thorpe*
"Any fucker can understand it" *Albert Einstein*
"Well it fucking looks like her" *Pablo Picasso*
"What fucking Iraqis?" *Emir of Kuwait*
"Who the fuck designed that?" *Prince Charles*
"Where the fuck did you come from?" *Doctor Livingstone*
"Fuck this for a game of soldiers!" *Colonel Oliver North*
"Does anyone fancy a fuck?" *Warren Beatty*
"How do you turn this fucking tap off?" *Archimedes*
"What fucking memoirs?" *John Major*

TRAVELLERS LOG

Right from the outset this project was conceived as a primary tool for the international globetrotter. I wanted it to be clear. I wanted it to be concise. Above all, I wanted it to be practical. That's the main reason why I've allowed ample space at the back of the book for you to make your own personal notations (another reason is that the publisher informed me, 3 days before we went to press, that I needed to stretch the text by a further 8 pages!). Anyhow, now you'll be able to include the address and phone number of your favourite restaurant or knocking shop and still have enough room for other useful foreign phrases like : "I'm not saying anything until I've spoken to my lawyer".

AUSTRALIA

AUSTRIA

BANGLADESH

BELGIUM

BRAZIL

BRUNEI

BULGARIA

CANADA

CHINA

DENMARK

EGYPT

ENGLAND

FINLAND

FRANCE

GERMANY

GREECE

HONG KONG

HUNGARY

INDIA

IRAN

IRAQ

IRELAND

ISRAEL

ITALY

JAMAICA

JAPAN

MEXICO

NETHERLANDS

NEW ZEALAND

NIGERIA

NORTHERN IRELAND

NORWAY

PAKISTAN

PERU

PHILLIPINES

POLAND

PORTUGAL

ROMANIA

RUSSIA

SAUDI ARABIA

SCOTLAND

SOUTH AFRICA

SPAIN

SWEDEN

TAIWAN

THAILAND

TURKEY

UKRAINE

USA

WALES

About the Author

Kelvin Birdseye was born in Brentwood, Essex in 1945 and educated at the local Secondary Modern. In his time, he has been a DJ, a market-trader and a used-car salesman, but for the past 20 years has worked for Premium Products plc of Basildon as International Sales Director. Mr Birdseye lives in a ranch-style bungalow in Brentwood with his fourth wife Tina. This is his first published work.

CAVEAT

Although a great deal of time and money has been spent on researching this book, the author regrets that he can accept no direct responsibility for the accuracy of the information contained herein. I mean who give a toss whether William Tell was Austrian or Swiss, and can anyone actually prove that I don't know the exact population of China? Sensitive souls may be offended by the frank and forthright nature of certain observations that I've made. But hey, if you can't take a joke you shouldn't have bought the fucker!